The Spirit of Corvallis
THE PACIFIC NORTHWEST'S MOST BEAUTIFUL TOWN

Copyright © 2008 by Corvallis Tourism

All rights reserved, including the right to reproduce this work in any form whatsoever without permission in writing from the publisher, except for brief passages in connection with a review. For information, please write:

The Donning Company Publishers
184 Business Park Drive, Suite 206
Virginia Beach, VA 23462

Steve Mull, General Manager
Barbara Buchanan, Office Manager
Faye Underwood, Editor
Lori Wiley, Graphic Designer
Derek Eley, Imaging Artist
Lori Porter, Project Research Coordinator
Scott Rule, Director of Marketing
Tonya Hannink, Marketing Coordinator

Dwight Tompkins, Project Director

Cataloging-in-Publication Data

The spirit of Corvallis / Edited by John Hope-Johnstone.
        p. cm.
     ISBN 978-1-57864-490-2 (hard cover : alk. paper)
     1. Corvallis (Or.)--Anecdotes. 2. Corvallis (Or.)--Pictorial works. 3. Corvallis (Or.)--Poetry. I. Hope-Johnstone, John.
     F884.C7S65 2008
     979.5'34--dc22
                                         2008005303

Printed in the United States of America at Walsworth Publishing Company

CONTENTS

6/Preface *by John Hope-Johnstone*
8/Welcome From the City of Corvallis—Sponsor
10/Autumn Sings *by Cindy Killip*
12/An Alternate Way to Explore *by Jean Marvell*
14/Are You Kidding Me? *by J. D. Mackenzie*
16/Barker-Uerlings Insurance—Sponsor
18/A Better Life *by Bob Harding*
20/Corvallis-OSU Symphony—Oldest in Oregon—Sponsor
22/The Best of Both Worlds *by Susan Shumway*
24/The Challenge of Corvallis *by Betty McCauley*
26/Coming Alive with Lifelong Learning *by Genny Lynch*
28/Two Cities with Heart! *by Alice Rampton*
30/Corvallis: It Started with Wonderful *by John Lopez Jr.*
32/A Crazy Quilt of Culture *by C. Lill Ahrens*
34/The Crows of Corvallis *by David Wodtke*
36/Cycling Heaven *by Tonya Claybaugh*
38/December 7th *by CMSgt Jeff Roy*
40/Finding My Calling in Corvallis *by Sheila Smith*
42/Four Paws Up for Corvallis *by Ange Crawford*
44/Giving From the Heart (of the Valley) *by Theresa Hogue*
46/Good Samaritan Regional Medical Center—Sponsor
48/The Great Coming Loose *by Steve Jones*
50/Hollywood Writer Dips Toes *by Linda Hamner*
52/In Corvallis, Art is Everywhere! *by Sara Swanberg*
54/A Kinder Climate *by Margaret Anderson*

56/A Little Bit of Wild *by Larina Warnock*
58/Look Up! *by Jill Allphin*
60/Oak Creek *by Natalie Daley*
62/Oh, No, You Go First *by Lee Lawton*
64/Oregon State University—Sponsor
68/The Power of Rivers *by Gregg Kleiner*
70/Praise Song in Five Stanzas *by Ann Staley*
72/Random Acts of Kindness *by Cristina White*
74/Real People *by Elizabeth Bennett*
76/Linn-Benton Community College—Sponsor
78/This Piece of This Valley *by Jana Zvibleman*
80/. . . Two! . . . One! . . . Go! *by Spencer Ahrens*
82/Starker Forests, Inc.—Sponsor
84/Weather *by Peg Mayo*
86/Willamette: First Communion *by Laurence P. Taoman*
88/Town & Country Realty—Sponsor
90/Words Enrich Our Lives Here *by Linda Gelbrich*
92/Corvallis at 150—Pacific Power—Sponsor
94/Corvallis, A Great Place for Kids *by Nancy Matsumoto*
98/Hewlett-Packard (HP) Corvallis Site—Sponsor
100/I Learned *by Melinda Stewart*
108/Photographer Contact Information
109/Sponsor Contact Information
110/Author Contact Information

The Spirit of Corvallis
PREFACE

We hope you will enjoy this *Spirit of Corvallis* book as much as we have enjoyed publishing it. This is not a history book. It is a snapshot of Corvallis in time, surrounding our Sesquicentennial year of 2007. It is part photographic book, part short essay book, and part poetry book. It is not contrived; it is quirky, defying classification; much like Corvallis itself; and that is just the way we wanted it.

"How dare you call Corvallis quirky!" a proud, red-faced citizen once chastised me.

"B-b-but," I stammered in reply, "what would you call a town that celebrates genius and invention as two of its major attributes?"

"But quirky is derogatory," he interjected.

"Not in my world," I responded. "In my world, it is a badge of honor, a crest of character."

Corvallis does have a quirky way of looking at life. This is a city that believes life should be gauged by quality, pace, and art, rather than by hustle and bustle. It is tempered by the juxtaposition of the world's computer giant and a world-class university. Yet, even with our Norman Rockwell-like look of an America many think lost, (and our great penchant for consensus), we get things done! As an example, *Harvard Business Review* stated that Corvallis was fifteenth in the nation for its creativity. *USA Today* reported that Corvallis' creativity has made it fourth in the nation for the number of patents, pouring forth from our many coffee shops, small businesses, Hewlett-Packard, and our wonderful Oregon State University. "There must be a brain trust going on in Corvallis," they stated.

We put together this legacy book with the help of our many sponsors, contributors, and friends. The Corvallis Photographic Guild and our finest professional photographers, along with the Corvallis & Benton County writers group and many other talented people were simply told: "Go to it, describe Corvallis." We didn't give out any writing or photographic assignments and sometimes the photographs and the essays will match and sometimes not, but they have all come from the heart and represent *The Spirit of Corvallis* in the soul of the writer or photographer.

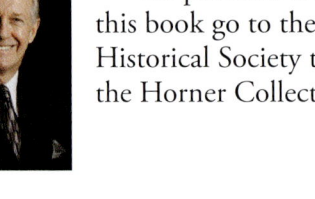

All proceeds from the sale of this book go to the Benton County Historical Society to create a home for the Horner Collection in Corvallis.

—*John Hope-Johnstone*
Corvallis Tourism
Editor

OSU baseball champs (by Dennis Wolverton)

Welcome From THE CITY OF CORVALLIS

Thou, too, sail on, O Ship of State!
Sail on, O Union, strong and great!
Humanity with all its fears,
With all the hopes of future years,

Henry Wadsworth Longfellow

We are a community filled "with all the hopes of future years." Travel with me around Corvallis and see our hopes for the next one hundred and fifty years.

Let's start at the Riverfront Commemorative Park, the heart of downtown. Looking at the Willamette River, we realize that Corvallis was born a river town and continues to honor and enjoy a salmon waterway and wildlife-filled riverbanks. Walking along Madison Avenue, we see people enjoying the bright sunshine, having coffee at our sidewalk cafés and browsing at a myriad of bookstores and retail shops. The downtown's future is bright: a local destination for eating, shopping and the arts.

The alley art along Madison Avenue draws us to The Arts Center, home to our thriving visual arts community. Across the Center's Plaza is Central Park, where people are playing Frisbee and, this evening, the Corvallis Community Band will play. Walking further, the Oregon State University campus is a center of student life, academic research, cultural arts, and PAC-10 sports. Linn-Benton Community College and the Corvallis School District also provide excellence in education. We are fortunate for our life-long learning opportunities.

This historic OSU campus forms the nucleus of our economic future; a vibrant local economy stimulated by university research. Corvallis is the heart of innovation in the Silicon Forest and the soul of entrepreneurial spirit. Our local economy sustains us into the future.

We catch a bus, passing the Benton County Health Department, and on toward the hill where much of our medical community resides. We are a regional medical center; augmenting our doctors and nurses is a rich fabric of non-profit service providers. Wellness is central to our way of life in the Pacific Northwest.

Returning to City Hall, we realize Corvallis is an engaged community; participating in local government issues and decisions, and volunteering for city boards and commissions and service clubs. Our truth: respect and caring for all people; similar or different, near or far.

Protecting the environment, a deep-seated community value, calls us to take the lightest footprints on our planet. We continue to minimize our impact on the environment—we want to be remembered for our contributions to environmental protection, and to the quality of life for future generations.

Lastly, Corvallis is home to safe, livable neighborhoods. Traveling around town, we see neighbors tending their gardens, painting their houses, and walking in their neighborhoods. Our community works with local partners to create affordable housing for current and future citizens.

I hope you enjoyed our trip—Corvallis is a special community. 'With all the hopes of future years,' may they be filled with peace and joy.

—Charlie Tomlinson
Mayor

City Hall (by Paul Rentz)

Autumn Sings in Corvallis
CINDY KILLIP

*a*s I step out my front door, a ragged V of migrating geese trumpets overhead. A friendly "hello" from a passing neighbor and a piercing caw from a crow complement the travelers' music. Within minutes I am strolling through one of many green spaces near the center of town—an autumn amphitheater surrounded by the foothills of the coastal mountain range. Blue sky breaks through the cloud cover, creating the perfect backdrop for the mosaic of gold and orange leaves and foggy mist that weaves gracefully through the treetops.

I wander along and take in a glorious breath, thinking about how fortunate I am to live here. The crisp air smells as fresh as it feels. I hear no revving engines or honking horns. No sirens. No people yelling. I am free to enjoy the music of autumn.

A squirrel chatters from a nearby tree while somewhere unseen a deer rustles in the underbrush. Bird melodies join the chorus and their song mixes with the harmony beneath my feet. *Crunch, crunch, shuffle*: The beats create a steady rhythm as I pass through leaves that have let go of their branches and carpeted the ground. Every so often, a soft *psplotch, psplotch* joins in as the rain-soaked earth catches and releases my boots.

Plink, plop, plink, plop, plink: A new rhythm quickly reaches a crescendo. The tapping of rain on the roof of leaves invites me to look up. The clouds have closed again, tucking Corvallis into the valley like a cozy blanket. I snuggle into my jacket and listen as they share their music with the song of autumn.

Cindy Killip is a publisher, writer, speaker, and exercise specialist who teaches and creates in Corvallis, Oregon. She is currently working on a book that offers solutions for managing osteoporosis and, since walking is a great exercise for building bone density, she takes advantage of all four seasons in Oregon.

Riverfront Park (by Paul Rentz)

An Alternative Way to Explore
JEAN MARVELL

There is much to discover in and around Corvallis. Exploring in a wheelchair is discovery in itself.

Roving the Corvallis area encourages artistic contemplation: rippling reflections in Marys River; lacey oaks silhouetted against fog; vibrant yellows and deep Kelly greens of fields and foliage; the rose garden in Avery Park. Or catching a glimpse of Marys Peak or The Three Sisters; or even wild turkeys, a doe, or a fawn.

I travel many bike and hiking paths in a motorized chair or scooter, equipped with outdoor tires. (Mine is called "Harley"). An able-bodied accompanist keeps me out of trouble most of the time.

Although I can tell about the time I nearly slipped from the trail into Croenmiller Lake in McDonald Forest and the time pine needles caused an unexpected slide down a slope at Bellfountain Park. Not all trails are consistently appropriate. Ask a hiker to check first.

Calmer experiences are available. Knocked down curbs in downtown Corvallis enable shopping. To venture further, there are wooded trails in dry weather. The boardwalk at Frazier Wetlands, a gentle trail through the Davis Farm or a paved bike path up Bald Hill are most enjoyable. McDonald Forest, an OSU Forestry Research project, offers trilliums, lupine, and camas in early spring. When we have almost forgotten the vibrant lime of sun-drenched moss or rain tears dancing on foliage, an afternoon on the Riverfront sidewalk downtown or on trails in Avery and Willamette Parks satisfies a longing. Within Benton County there are also: Finley Wildlife Preserve, Beazel Park, Camp Adair nature preserve, a path at Tyee Winery, and others I have yet to discover.

Adventure! Enjoy! It will prompt you to poetry.

We moved to Corvallis in 1948 after my husband, Elliot Marvell, had completed a Ph.D. in chemistry at the University of Illinois and was hired to teach at Oregon Agricultural College. I took courses to complete my B.S. degree, but since I was a liberal arts major, offerings were limited. (University of Oregon was the only university in Oregon.) Later I obtained training as a visual artist and have taught adult education at Corvallis Art Center, Linn-Benton Community College, and the Crafts Center at OSU.

I have been an active artist since the 1970s. My work is included in The Encyclopedia of Paper Making & Bookbinding *by Reimer-Epp and Reimer, Running Press, Philadelphia & London, 2002 and in* Paper Art *by Diane Maurer-Mathison, Watson Guptill 1997. Recently my book art has been placed in a number of libraries and museums. I have exhibited art work in the United States, Europe, and South Korea.*

We raised a daughter, Linnnaea, and a son, Kristan in Corvallis. They attended Harding and Jefferson grammar schools, Highland View Junior High School (now Linus Pauling Middle School), and the old Corvallis High School. Except for two sabbatical years in Switzerland we have lived in the home we built on Alta Vista Drive since 1960. At that time it was a dirt road on the county line.

Winter farm near Conifer and Highway 20 (by Jonathan Brownell, Blue Castle Photography)

Are You Kidding Me?
J. D. MACKENZIE

Corvallis, special? Please. Try Tahoe or Jackson or Friday Harbor. You probably wouldn't like it here.

So you think you might enjoy living next to a major university for all of the cultural and commercial advantages? We have one right here, but see how you like it when your cute little town is invaded by twenty thousand aliens every September. Most of them wearing iPods and visible underwear. Repeat after me: "Get off my lawn!"

Don't believe everything you read. For a place with so much rain, we're running out of water.

The arts are supposed to be thriving here, but only if you like the rhythm and blues, alternative, symphony, and live theater. Sorry to disappoint you, but there's no opera.

We don't have ocean beaches, ski resorts, or whitewater. You'll have to travel at least an hour to get to those.

Don't look too closely at the regional economic data. We have among the most expensive housing costs in the state. And there's the lowest unemployment rate, but what that really means is that if you're an employer, you're just going to have to try harder and pay more to find good help.

If you like shopping in big box stores, keep driving. Most of what we have are unique, independently owned businesses with great customer service.

We're the volunteer capital of Oregon. Big deal. Does the world really need any more do-gooders?

Okay, so the wine and microbrews here are outstanding. But there's a downside: the good stuff is in high demand, and you know what demand does to price.

Did you know that Athens has 320 sunny days each year? It does. We don't.

Please don't come here. We're miserable. Can't you tell?

J. D. Mackenzie writes short fiction, creative non-fiction, and recently some pretty bad poetry. A fourth generation Corvallisite, his work has been published in The Community College Moment, The Broadside, Eugene Weekly, Corvallis Gazette-Times, *and several student publications. He chairs the continuing education department at a community college in western Oregon.*

Art Center Statue (by Mike Bergen)

Barker-Uerlings Insurance
SPONSOR

The very spirit of community and goodwill in Corvallis is embodied in Barker-Uerlings Insurance.

Barker-Uerlings was originally two separate Independent Insurance Agencies; Porter-Haaland Insurance, founded in 1911, and Cecil Barker Insurance, founded in1913. After a merger, Barker-Uerlings has grown into the thriving Corvallis business it is today; a full service insurance agency with twenty employees and a great sense of community. The agency has a long history of contributing to Corvallis through employee involvement and financial sponsorship of community events. Cecil Barker was mayor of Corvallis, and his son Terry is a former member of city council. Current owner Steve Uerlings continues this tradition with several employees serving as board members to various civil and nonprofit organizations. Barker-Uerlings has participated in and sponsored such creative and interesting events as United Way's "Rock the Cradle of Jazz" jazz concert fundraiser, Boys and Girls Club's "Rubber Ducky Derby," The Corvallis Clinic Foundation "Putting on the Pink" fashion show, and the Good Samaritan Hospital Foundation's "Physicians Gourmet Faire." For several years Barker-Uerlings coordinated the collection, cleaning, and distribution of winter coats for underprivileged children in Corvallis. This kind of self-directed philanthropy is a prime example of their dedication to the community of Corvallis.

Located in the heart of the city directly across from the fire station, Barker-Uerlings selected this location to be a focal point in the community. In planning for the new location they made sure their conference room could be used by civic and non-profit organizations as a boardroom, and they supply coffee and refreshments for the groups. Not only does the insurance agency see the benefits in enriching the Corvallis community today; they understand the importance of history and are contributing members of the Benton County Historical Society.

Their cornerstone is the constant and continued employee civic involvement for almost a hundred years and their effort to give back to the community they serve. They have thrived with culture and pride, while enriching Corvallis as a whole and helping us become a more vibrant community. Their dedication to make Corvallis a better place is what makes Barker-Uerlings Insurance truly a gem of the Corvallis community.

Steve Uerlings

Corvallis scene (by Paul Rentz)

A Better Life
BOB HARDING

i am the youngest of four children, and life wasn't going well for our family before our move to Corvallis in 1974. My dad had decided to pursue other options in life, leaving my mother alone to raise her four children. I remember the first time I heard of Corvallis. I was six years old and we were moving from Orchards, Washington. My mother had just taken a job at Oregon State University and we were excited to get a new start. I remember helping pack up our U-Haul and heading to our destination in what seemed to me such a faraway city. As we crossed the Interstate Bridge, I clearly remember her saying: "We are in Oregon now and our lives are going to be better." Our lives did change. Corvallis offered me friends, sports, and activities. Between school, Cub Scouts, Boys and Girls Club, Beaver football, and the YMCA, I had everything a kid needed. I have friends I speak with daily that I met in Ms. Mimnaugh's first grade class the first day I attended Garfield School. To me, Corvallis is not just a city, it's a community and will always have a special place in my heart. My whole family lives here and I visit as often as I can. The day we crossed the bridge into Oregon, heading for Corvallis, was the luckiest day of my life.

Bob came to Corvallis in 1974 and attended Garfield, Highland View, Corvallis High, Linn-Benton Community College, and Oregon State University. He has been in the banking industry for fourteen years and currently works in Portland. He is the youngest of four and his siblings, nieces and nephews, and mother live in Corvallis. He is an avid Beaver football fan and rarely misses a game. He visits Corvallis often and it will always be "home" to him.

Beavers Football (by Dennis Wolverton)

Corvallis-OSU Symphony—Oldest in Oregon

SPONSOR

"Great Music for a Great Community" is more than just a motto. It has become everyone's expectation for the Corvallis-OSU Symphony Orchestra.

Now in its 102nd season, the longest continually-operating orchestra in the state is a major force in the cultural life of the mid-Willamette Valley. From its inception in 1906 as a collegiate orchestra composed of nine members, the symphony has grown into a highly regarded, eighty-member ensemble performing at least six major concerts each season. Distinguished soloists from around the world complement the musical artistry of faculty, community members, and students along with about fifty professional musicians from Portland, Salem, Eugene, and Corvallis.

Concerts are held in the twelve hundred seat Austin Auditorium of the LaSells Stewart Center on the Oregon State University campus. Community members serve on the Symphony Society Board, on committees, and as ushers for the concerts. Private donations, an Endowment Fund, and local businesses provide support for the orchestra. The Corvallis-OSU Symphony is truly a community treasure.

Please visit www.symphony.peak.org for more information.

Corvallis-OSU Symphony Maestro Marlan Carlson.

102-year-old Corvallis-OSU Symphony.

The Best of Both Worlds
SUSAN SHUMWAY

Long a denizen of East Coast cultural environments, moving to Corvallis in the mid-1970s was something akin to falling off the edge of the planet. Hamburger and pizza joints studded the town, good eating didn't exist, and "art" was confined to Eugene. Corvallis was a university town rooted in agriculture, engineering, and the sciences, and culture was something found in a Petri dish.

I contented myself with wandering the many hiking trails in the area and learned to love the natural tangled beauty of the riverbanks and the ancient oaks in the deep mossy forests. I was so immersed in discovering nature that I almost missed the revolution happening in the streets.

I first became aware of it when art galleries began popping up like seeds in spring. And, miracle of miracles, we got an Italian restaurant, a French restaurant, and good food was everywhere. Coffee shops and bakeries moved into old buildings, and tables and chairs began edging onto sidewalks, changing the ambience of downtown. People took time to have a leisurely cup of soup or tea and visit with friends, creating an atmosphere not unlike Parisian cafés. Even the riverfront was tamed, becoming a mecca for families and anyone needing a nature break from their workday.

In the long, lazy rays of a sunny autumn day in 2007, I realized that I no longer needed to hop on a plane to find the cultural things that feed the soul and brighten the spirit. I have it all, nature and culture, right here in Corvallis.

Susan Shumway grew up near Washington, D.C., but has lived in Corvallis for over thirty years. Believing that both art and nature are important for health and well-being, she works with dialysis patients using writing as a therapeutic and creative tool under the auspices of ArtsCare. She and her husband Bill own Pegasus Art Gallery and feel fortunate to be members of a remarkably talented community of artists in all media. In her spare time, she volunteers with Benton Hospice, Habitat for Humanity, and the Corvallis Public Library, and writes with the help of three critique groups. She is the mother of five and grandmother of eleven.

Corvallis nightlife (by Dennis Wolverton)

The Challenge of Corvallis
BY BETTY MCCAULEY

*i*t's a joy and a challenge to live in Corvallis where the community doesn't take joy for granted. Here a willing population takes responsibility for building and preserving treasures. We trace our beloved Corvallis-Benton County Public Library to a meeting of the Woman's Club over a century ago. They raised money to buy four books (including *Pilgrim's Progress)* for the volunteer firemen—the beginning of a fine library collection. Corvallis built the first beautiful building, and later Benton County joined in support. This community enthusiastically raised money twice for additions. A library that checks out a million and a half items a year deserves a home of utility and beauty.

That's why I love Corvallis. Citizens with visions rally the people to make them realities. We're a college town. As Oregon Agricultural College grew into the present Oregon State University, creative people in town saw the need for a center to celebrate the arts. When the Episcopal congregation built a larger church, the *Gazette-Times* bought the old one for the land. They sold the charming old church to Corvallis for one dollar, if the city would move it. The historic old building is now The Arts Center, with a full program of exhibits, art education, musical events, and poetry readings.

The community supports organizations of enrichments for the young and old—the Osborn Aquatic Center, the Boys and Girls Club, the Historical Museum in Philomath, a future museum along Riverfront Park, and others. Even the elderly and disabled have Grace Center for Adult Day Services, a place of love and dignity, because everyone deserves a share of Corvallis joy.

In fifty-six years since coming to Corvallis, I've had the joy and satisfaction of serving on all three library boards. My marine biologist husband Jim helped renovate the Barn Theater (precursor to the Majestic). I was on the first Arts Center board and have been a board member for Grace Center for Adult Services since its dream stage. Our children and grandchildren thrived in Corvallis Schools. No wonder I love this town.

The Arts Center (by Paul Rentz)

Coming Alive With Lifelong Learning
GENNY LYNCH

Corvallis has caught me in its web of learning and I'm delighted.

First I took formal classes: stained glass at OSU craft center to finish an old project, writing a memoir at Parks and Recreation, computer skills at Linn-Benton. Perhaps I'd get an advanced degree or Internet date.

Feeling low I went "Walking with the Doc" who discussed health issues while we were aerobic. Pilates enabled me to do a rollup for the first time. An unexpected benefit of commando crawls was the ability to open jars with ease.

Lessons are everywhere! Classes at the co-op grocery taught me to cook unusual grains. Quinoa anyone? I lunched at the libraries "Paperbag" lectures and learned how to compost. My bank's seminars on credit, car buying, and retirement investing improved my financial fitness.

Unexpected teachers are everywhere. I don't try to escape. Clients demonstrate layering watercolor and pruning bonsai trees. While hiking with a soils scientist I learn about the dirt clogging our boot treads. Further along the trail an iridescent orange ooze sparks a passionate conversation about slime mold research and its benefits to mankind. I still won't touch it!

Sometimes lessons are piggybacked. At life drawing as I sketched his languid pose our nude model told us how to construct a mud house.

Then I discovered you didn't need a partner to take a dance class. Contra, square, round, swing, and amazingly, I'm fulfilling a fantasy. I'm being whirled and twirled to a zydeco waltz. It's effortless and exhilarating.

If I wasn't afraid of catching my hair on fire I'd attempt fire dancing. Instead I think I'll go watch a tsunami experiment at the OSU wave tank.

Genny Lynch is interested in almost everything. She's working, dancing, and continuing to learn while writing her first book.

Corvallis Ballet School (by Judith Waring Smith of Alsea)

Two Cities with Heart!
ALICE RAMPTON

On March 27, 1992, at Corvallis City Hall, Mayor Emil Landovsky of Uzhgorod, Ukraine and Corvallis Mayor Charlie Vars signed an agreement which created an official sister city relationship between Uzhgorod, Ukraine and Corvallis, Oregon, USA.

This relationship flourished under the efforts of volunteers in both cities. During the next fifteen years, nearly one thousand citizens traveled between the two cities on delegations including government officials, high school students, teachers, business leaders, artists, doctors, nurses, therapists, dentists, university professors, librarians, engineers, social workers, choirs, musicians, search and rescue specialists, agri-business owners, and others.

In 1999, Corvallis volunteers sent the first of five shipments of humanitarian aid to Uzhgorod, as the country was experiencing instability with high inflation and unemployment. Over two hundred fifty thousand pounds of aid was included in these "Aid to Uzhgorod" shipments, which helped equip several hospitals and clinics, a rehabilitation center for children with disabilities, a mammography center, and a computer lab at Uzhgorod National University. In 2001, The TOUCH Project (Take One Ukrainian Child's Hand) was established under the direction of the Corvallis-Uzhgorod Sister Cities Association and provided additional support for children in need in Uzhgorod.

The relationship between Uzhgorod and Corvallis is symbolic of the outreach and spirit of volunteerism that citizens in Corvallis have valued through the years. There is no paid staff involved with the Corvallis-Uzhgorod Sister Cities Association. This esprit de corps effort was awarded in 2001, when Corvallis received the "Best Overall Program Award" in the world from Sister Cities International for cities with populations between fifty thousand and one hundred thousand.

Alice Henderson Rampton was born and raised in Corvallis, Oregon, attending Harding Elementary, Western View, and Corvallis High School. She graduated from the University of Oregon and taught school in Beaverton, Oregon before devoting the subsequent decades to volunteerism and raising six children with her spouse, Mark. She has been involved with Safety Town, the Boys and Girls Club, Corvallis-Uzhgorod Sister Cities Association, Benton County Historical Society, American Field Service, and co-chairs a non-profit organization entitled The TOUCH Project (Take One Ukrainian Child's Hand).

Uzhgorod Dancers (by Paul Kline)

Corvallis: It Started with Wonderful
JOHN LOPEZ JR.

funny how things stay with you. I remember how the rain stopped and the clouds parted as I rode my fully loaded touring bike slowly past the "Corvallis City Limits" sign on Philomath Boulevard. It was the first day of my Newport, Oregon to Boston, Massachusetts trip on U.S. Route 20 and it had been rainy and cold since leaving the coast. Corvallis is still etched in my memory—dry, warm and just plain WONDERFUL.

Years later, seeking a community in which to relocate, I returned to Corvallis for a closer look. I found the central business district compact and prosperous. A contender for any "Main Street U.S.A." competition. The Benton County Courthouse, built in the 1870s, still presides over downtown and the Avery-Helm Historic District southwest of city center is a tribute to preserving the past. I discovered that Corvallis actually encircles the campus of Oregon State University where the immense greensward called Lower Campus serves as a transition from cityscape to the studied profile of academia.

Exploring the hinterlands I found comfortable neighborhoods near schools, churches, parks, medical services, and commercial zones. There are high-tech enterprises here, too: software development, applied bio-science, and engineering firms. A definite entrepreneurial nod to the future. Corvallis actively promotes two-wheel transportation as a bicycle-friendly city where bike lanes and bikeways abound. Compact metro buses provide a mass transit system on a decidedly human scale. I read a newspaper editorial about the city's growth boundary and can't help but agree with the writers that in an agricultural river valley it is a good thing to establish limits for urban growth.

City folk tell me of an active citizenry, a responsive local government and hometown pride. I am attracted to what flourishes here—art and science, the pursuit of knowledge, respect for the past, plans for the future, outdoor recreational opportunities, the protection of the natural environment.

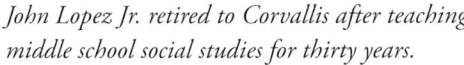

Corvallis. The city that was wonderfully warm to me one June afternoon is still wonderful—I call Corvallis home. I've even learned to appreciate a few drops of chilling rain now and then!

John Lopez Jr. retired to Corvallis after teaching middle school social studies for thirty years.

County courthouse (by Paul Rentz)

A Crazy Quilt of Culture
C. LILL AHRENS

Twenty years ago I was an artist who could no longer do art. I yearned to, but my muse had been burned out by a lonely and competitive art career. Then I moved with my husband and son from Colorado to Oregon via South Korea. I arrived in Corvallis with a spanking new writing muse, eager to write about our crazy overseas sojourn. I just needed to learn how.

A Benton Center creative writing class was my portal to a kind of arts community I'd never known was possible; it was extremely supportive of the muse. While I learned to write, my husband learned to perform improv, our son learned to design kinetic sculpture vehicles, and my art muse rose from its ashes. We all took part in the annual Community Art Show: anyone, young or old, professional or amateur, could contribute work in any medium, transforming the Art Center's upscale gallery into a dazzling, floor-to-ceiling, crazy quilt of art, of amazing overall quality.

Corvallis itself is a crazy quilt of the arts—musical, theatrical, botanical, whimsical, and many more—which can result in some interesting juxtapositions. For example, the Chocolate Fantasy is a culinary competition in the midst of a fund-raising auction of local art; daVinci Days is a celebration of engineering, music, science, film, kinetic sculpture racing, and children's sidewalk art; businesses of all kinds double as year-round galleries for local artists.

Corvallis is a community whose artists support one another; a city of entertainers who love to be entertained. It's a town with what I call high CPC (Culture Per Capita). A crazy quilt of culture.

C. Lill Ahrens is a published, award-winning artist and author, a writer's coach, book doctor, and a creative writing instructor for Corvallis Parks and Recreation and Linn-Benton Community College, where she passes on the supportive philosophy.

Corvallis Dance (by Dennis Wolverton)

The Crows of Corvallis
DAVID WODTKE

"If men had wings and bore black feathers, few of them would be clever enough to be crows." —Henry Ward Beecher

The crows of Corvallis are well fed and stick together, like the people. Not that crows elsewhere don't, or people for that matter. But there is an ingenuity about this place, a sense of innovation and abundance, like anything is possible. Like magic. It's practical magic. Like when the walnuts are ripe up near Walnut Boulevard the crows get together with all their relations and drop them onto a neighborhood street, then wait for passing cars to crack them open for lunch. Crows are like that. They see a possibility and make it real. They don't spend all day cawing and croaking about it.

Over sixty years ago four men back from "The War" took up the crow standard. An engineering professor and three of his students set up shop over the old Rexall drug store and set to work "cracking nuts" in their own way to put dinner on the table. CH2M HILL grew and continues to join with other firms all over the world—and like the crows can pretty much figure a way to crack any tough nut from environmental cleanup to road design, from water treatment to oil extraction. Like many others in Corvallis and the world today, this flock focuses on getting things done in a sound, sustainable way.

Expand the Panama Canal you say? No problem. Clear and redesign a city for the Olympics? Doesn't ruffle our feathers much. That's just how people are here in Corvallis. We learned it from the crows.

David Wodtke loves to walk the streets of Corvallis as well as the hills and beaches of the surrounding countryside. When he's not working as an analyst he enjoys writing poetry, journaling, listening to music, and playing bassoon in local groups. Gardening and meditation are two other passions that help him keep a healthy balance.

Chestnut trees in winter on Highway 20 (by L. Dyer)

Cycling Heaven
TONYA CLAYBAUGH

Cycling is enjoyed by many in Corvallis. This is a refreshing alternative to the fast-paced drive of other cities. This city lends itself to viewing in its entirety.

At first you notice the green growth of nature, as well as the creative talent and industry which springs from its tree-lined streets. You can discover interesting places that can supply you with what you may need.

Continuing, you will also discover the remains of what was. Corvallis turns a solemn grey in memory of industry and individuals who gave until they were gone. Buildings, parks, and grants pasted onto another generation, each of these reflecting the lifestyles of the era past.

Corvallis does not end the opportunity to continue cycling. It gathers incentive from the past and shifts into a new fire red vitality. Entrepreneurship revives and builds new futures, while respecting the foundation it already has.

Each cycle reveals another vista and perspective to what we call home.

Mid Williamette Valley Bicycle Club

Walking to OSU (by Cristina White)

December 7th
C.M. SGT. JEFF ROY

Any book celebrating a moment in time during their sesquicentennial of 2007 cannot ignore the men and women in the armed forces overseas.

It's December 7th here in Kuwait
Our flag is at half mast
It's Friday
Spaghetti and meatballs for lunch

It's December 7th here in Kuwait
Yea that day
End of the week
Fish for dinner

It's December 7th here in Kuwait
The day that would live in infamy
A generation ago
A lifetime almost gone

It's December 7th here in Kuwait
Across the tarmac I see the Japanese compound
No longer an enemy, No longer a threat
But my comrade and friend we stand together

It's December 7th here in Kuwait
I stand as the gateway
Born of the last great generation
Father of the next

Oh how I wish they could know one another
Grandfathers and grandmothers
Be proud
Grandsons and granddaughters
Be proud

It's December 7th here in Kuwait
Our flag is at half mast…..

By CMSgt Jeff Roy
Ali Al Salem Air Base, Kuwait

The Crossed Swords of Baghdad

Finding My Calling in Corvallis
SHEILA SMITH

After a divorce booted me out of my faculty wife sinecure, I was willing to do anything to stay in my beloved Corvallis. I tried nude modeling for the OSU Art Department but it was too cold.

So I packed chickens at a local egg farm. The barn was straight out of Dickens: twenty-watt bulb, air thick with dust from the dirt floor, feathers, and droppings. We packers took the chickens from the catchers—upside down by their feet so they wouldn't struggle—and carried them to the stuffers who forced them into crates to be ferried to their probable fate as nuggets.

Next, I became the keeper of OSU's cockroach zoo. The collection comprised about fifty kinds of cockroach, housed by species in round two-and-a-half gallon cartons with a smear of petroleum jelly inside the rim. Being too fastidious to get their feet sticky, the bugs didn't escape. Each species had its characteristic stink—somewhere between rotting garbage and unwashed socks.

Then, I collected rumen fluid, a sludge of feed and digestive juices from a cow's second stomach, or rumen. I'd pull on a veterinary obstetric glove to my elbow, uncork the plexiglass tube implanted into the cow, pray she wouldn't burp through it, insert my arm, and grab a sample. Despite vigorous scrubbing, the manure-silage reek clung to my skin for hours.

Finally, Social Security let me stop scrounging a living to stay in Corvallis. That's when I discovered my true calling—dog training.

Rambunctious animals become well-mannered companions and the worst that happens is puppy piles.

Sheila Smith is a professional dog trainer and amateur writer who has sustained herself in Corvallis since 1960.

Benton County Fair (by Paul Rentz)

Four Paws Up for Corvallis
ANGE CRAWFORD

My best friend has a tail. Lest you worry he's a genetic throwback, rest assured Fernando is pure Lotta-Some—a lotta this; some o' that. Unlike me, he's tall, dark, and gorgeous, though perhaps a bit hirsute.

We were introduced by matchmakers at Heartland Humane Society. Four years later, Fernando and I still begin each day with a jog in one of Corvallis' off-leash parks. He does a six-minute mile and I don't, leaving him time to examine and sort treasures along the trail. Because he's a collector, I'm forced to cull the morning's valuables to those easily carried. Fernando's definition of "carry" includes dragging.

On weekends when Fernando feels the urge to practice his dog paddle, we head for Willamette Park. The pulsing river and glimpses of ducks, osprey, and the occasional beaver never fail to enthrall me. I pull out binoculars and bird-watch while Fernando explores the eddies for specimens to add to his stick collection.

Evenings after work, we often stop by Martin Luther King Jr. Park to explore the year-round creek. To Fernando's amazement, city planners located the creek right next to the baseball field so errant balls land in the shallows. He selects one and we go downtown to a sidewalk café where the bartender serves up local brew and a large bowl of water. Friends arrive and we listen to live music until Fernando pointedly rises and picks up his ball.

Back home, we curl up in front of the fire—kept blazing with sticks from Fernando's collection.

I reflect that, like Fernando, Corvallis is a Lotta-Some—a lotta great people and some o' the best-protected nature sites anywhere.

Ange Crawford lives and writes in Corvallis. Her work appears in magazines, journals, anthologies, and newspapers worldwide. She was recently honored by Oregon Writers' Colony for her nonfiction.

Parker Creek at Marys Peak (by Dennis Wolverton)

Giving from the Heart (of the Valley)
THERESA HOGUE

*e*very community has its handful of philanthropists who make it their priority to return some of their hard-earned dollars to their beloved town. Corvallis has more than its share of beneficent benefactors—people like Mario Pastega or Ruth and Jim Howland—whose names are attached to worthy projects across the community.

Many Corvallis residents will never have their name on a sports arena, but our neighbors pull together time and time again to help their neighbors in need. As a reporter, I am often responsible for writing articles about folks who have fallen on hard times. Sometimes it's a family displaced by a fire; at other times it's parents facing the ultimate nightmare, discovering their child has a terminal illness.

No matter how many of these stories I write, and in the last seven years it has been an astonishing number, it never ceases to amaze me how people immediately and enthusiastically respond. And the generosity is not just financial. While many millions of dollars have been raised in our town for numerous worthy causes, so too have needs been met by volunteers who step up to do any task asked of them. Many will remember the disappearance of Brooke Wilberger as a galvanizing event, which brought together people from all walks of life to search for her.

The volunteers who recently helped build a dream house for Boey Byers and her family is yet another example of this kind of altruistic behavior our town residents often exhibit, and there are plenty of other examples that never get that kind of media attention, but are just as worthy of our praise. The men and women who volunteer in the SMART program, for instance, spending an hour a week reading with children who truly need one-on-one adult support, are a great example.

In a world where we are faced at every turn with environmental, social, and health crises, it is heartwarming to be reminded of the ways in which people continue to reach out to strangers with open hearts and open arms. The spirit of Corvallis is truly a generous one.

Theresa Hogue is the features reporter at the Corvallis Gazette-Times, *and has been with the paper for more than seven years. She was born and raised in Portland, and has lived most of her life in the state. Hogue is a graduate of Portland State University. She lives with her partner, Joseph, her choodle Emma and her cat Lulu in a small bungalow in northwest Corvallis.*

Sunrise over Corvallis (by Jeff Watkins)

Good Samaritan Regional Medical Center
A BRIEF HISTORY

The story of Good Samaritan Regional Medical Center stretches back to the mid-1800s, when the streets of Corvallis were still unpaved, Oregon was still a territory at the end of a trail, and medicine often meant a shot of whiskey for what ailed you.

As health care evolved from home-based hospitals and "doctor shops" above local banks and stores, the first Corvallis Hospital was established at 21st and Monroe in 1913. A larger Corvallis General, funded by private investors, opened in 1922, but by 1948 had fallen upon hard times and was nearly bankrupt.

A group of community leaders, including Starker Forests founder T. J. Starker and Episcopal Rector Reverend Charles Neville, successfully raised enough funds to buy out the remaining investors and reconstitute the hospital as a not-for-profit, community-based facility affiliated with the Episcopal Diocese of Oregon.

Since that time, the hospital's location changed again, from its long-time site at NW 27th and Harrison to its current 84-acre campus north of town. That facility opened in 1975, and numerous medical office buildings and specialty services soon followed.

Today, Good Samaritan Regional Medical Center is the flagship of a five-hospital regional health system, Samaritan Health Services. Housed in Corvallis are regional services including a cardiovascular institute, comprehensive cancer center, inpatient mental health services, and one of Oregon's three Level 2 trauma centers. Good Samaritan and its affiliated hospitals and physician clinics provide family-wage jobs for thousands of area residents, and Samaritan Health Services is among the region's largest employers.

Good Samaritan has received state and national recognition for quality, and four times has been named to *Oregon Business* magazine's list of Oregon's Top 100 Employers.

Corvallis fields (by Greg Lief)

The Great Coming Loose
STEVE JONES

Walking about, I find self-tapping, sheetrock, and brass
screws, ring-shank nails, green sinkers, hollow-rivets, and
    upholstery tacks
lodged in sidewalk cracks and asphalt seams.
I imagine the great coming loose, the disassembly and
    deconstruction—
the untimely and ongoing parting at joints.
How a mechanic's best efforts with counter-clockwise
or tapered aircraft threads fail to keep the halves together.
Our stuff falls apart as we use it.
I find the evidence—a haphazard trail of
    fasteners
and chuckle at this persistent dissolution.
Backyard mechanics be on guard—your best
    efforts are never done.
Arm yourselves with Yankee screwdrivers
    and ash-handled
monkey wrenches for tightening continuously loosening
    fasteners—
threads that migrate from thirty or forty pounds of
    torque,
to mere hand-tight, to falling away by Murphy's Law—
to be picked up by a sharp-eyed jack-of-all-trades,
who stores artifacts in empty coffee tins.
Who knows when you might need a spare galvanized
    lynch-pin?

Steve Jones is a retired high school writing teacher, who coaches student teachers at Oregon State and Willamette University. Every July he gathers with twenty K-12 teachers to write and exchange best teaching practices in the four week Oregon Writing Project at Willamette University Summer Institute. Steve and his partner, Ana Maria, husband a long-term tree farm on Decker Road south of Corvallis.

Riverfront Art (by Jeff Watkins)

Hollywood Writer Dips Toes in Corvallis Literary Pond
LINDA ELIN HAMNER

i loved being a Hollywood writer. The pay was good and I enjoyed being in the company of other writers; they are always the smartest people in the room. We had spirited conversations about everything—except, of course, the actual stories and screenplays we were currently writing. We skulked around, paranoid and suspicious. We were convinced everyone was trying to suck the ideas out of our brains, leaving our heads as empty as gourds.

I wrote screenplays in my darkened office, drapes drawn. I was even wary of my cat, Cleo, who exhibited an unnatural interest in the pages that spewed out of my printer. Why was she trying to get her grubby little paws on them? She was up to no good, I was sure of it. She was a cat of dubious moral character.

When my husband and I retired to Corvallis, I desperately wanted to connect with other writers. I saw an announcement for the Writers Workroom at LBCC's Benton Center and jumped at the chance to sign up. I looked forward to spirited conversations about everything—except, of course, the current stories we were writing.

Imagine my surprise when I walked into the first meeting and people were actually reading their stories. Out loud! For everyone to hear! Lill Ahrens, the instructor, had created a safe haven for writers. There was neither treachery nor skullduggery afoot. In Corvallis, not only are writers the smartest people in the room, they're also the most supportive, creative, and honorable.

If I were writing a screenplay, it is at exactly this point I'd write "The MUSIC SWELLS and a golden, celestial light bathes the classroom."

Linda Hamner, an Emmy-award-winning TV writer, is also the co-author of Letters from Cleo and Tyrone *(St. Martin's Press.) She is currently working on her second novel,* Boobs over Hollywood, *and is teaching a screenwriting course at Linn-Benton Community College's Benton Center.*

Pullman at Depot Suites (by Mike Bergen)

In Corvallis, Art is Everywhere!
SARA SWANBERG

in 2007 nearly two hundred Corvallis cultural organizations appeared on an incomplete list compiled by a local nonprofit. From the well-established Corvallis Community Band to the brand spankin' new Willamette Stage, citizens of this energetic town actively support the arts with all levels of participation. Knowing this made it easy to accept the offer to become the new director of The Arts Center in Corvallis.

Economically a science-oriented community, Corvallis citizens understand the strong relationship between the arts and sciences. Lifelong experiences in the arts have resulted in more innovative engineers, doctors, and teachers. The plethora of ongoing opportunities available in this relatively small community means that scientists are also photographers and painters; doctors are musicians; and artists show up in all circles.

Taking a walk on a fall afternoon or summer evening, I can hear bands, orchestra, and choral groups performing on stages throughout the city, in parks, and within every indoor venue imaginable. Theater productions emerge in brand-new facilities such as the Corvallis High School theater and continue in the more seasoned venues such as the Majestic and on OSU's campus. Opera is heard filtering out of windows, and people are learning tap, ballet, tango, samba, and swing all over town. Artists' and writers' critique groups meet in private homes and in coffee houses. Active Corvallis Art Guilds focus on the visual arts, fiber arts, woodworking, ceramics, and photography.

An extraordinary number of local artists continue to exhibit their work in Corvallis. Take a stroll downtown and visit Pegasus Gallery and several smaller artist cooperative galleries. Visit the historic Arts Center, Fairbanks Gallery, LaSells Stewart Center, open studios, and local businesses. Art is everywhere!

Corvallis children can start early with impressive school music programs, Heart of the Valley Children's Choir, various student jazz groups, classes at The Arts Center, as well as artist residencies in some schools. Children can continue their arts and culture experiences in the summer with Globetrotters Arts & Culture Camp, at OSU's Kid Spirit and the Craft Center, with Parks & Recreation activities, as well as myriad private opportunities.

We all come together annually to celebrate the arts at the Corvallis Fall Festival and the da Vinci Days Festival. And as we celebrate our 150th with speeches, parades, music, murals, and fireworks, Corvallis revels in its truly fine state of the arts.

The current director of The Arts Center of Corvallis, Sara Swanberg has enjoyed a lifetime in the arts as a teacher, clay artist, musician, and film producer. A one-time studio artist, Swanberg turned her sights to the important work of arts administration beginning in the late 80s, focusing strictly on arts education for fifteen years.

Corvallis Dancers (by Dennis Wolverton)

A Kinder Climate
MARGARET ANDERSON

*i*n the fall of 1962, my husband Norm was offered a position at OSU. At the time, we were living in eastern Canada, where spring is the season of mud and summers are hot and humid. But it was winter that wore me down—shoveling snow drifts with frozen fingers, skidding on icy roads, and forever stuffing the resisting, squirming bodies of our three-year-old twins into snowsuits and fur-lined boots.

When we explained to people we were moving to a place with a kinder climate, they laughed at us! That October, newspapers were full of pictures of Oregon—flattened forests and barns reduced to matchsticks by the Columbus Day storm.

As it turned out, the storm opened the way for us to become part of our new community. Soon after arriving, we showed up for a work party in Avery Park. The twins, happily clad in raincoats and tennis shoes, helped drag away broken Douglas fir branches bigger than themselves.

When crocuses and daffodils ushered in spring, followed by avenues of blossoming cherry trees and a riot of rhododendrons, I knew that this was where I wanted to be. Then came summer with sun-drenched days and cool, breezy evenings. The bright colors of fall were finally muted by gray winter skies, but the occasional sun break always held a promise of spring.

And that's why we're still here forty-five years later. Sure, I've been known to complain about the rain. But with its tree-lined streets reflecting the changing seasons, Corvallis has a climate that is hard to beat.

I grew up in Scotland, and came to Corvallis by way of Canada, when my husband Norm joined the faculty of the Entomology Department at OSU in 1962. I have written children's books over the years while raising four children. I enjoy reading, gardening, and grandchildren—not necessarily in that order.

Holiday Inn Express on the river (by Jonathan Brownell, Blue Castle Photography)

A Little Bit of Wild
LARINA WARNOCK

The first time we stepped onto the boardwalk at the Jackson-Frazier Wetlands, the scent of fallen fruit wafted toward us on an August breeze. "What kind of plant is that?" my youngest daughter asked.

"That's a fern," my husband told her.

Our two middle children skipped ahead of us while I pushed my youngest son's wheelchair. Behind, our teenage daughter moped forward on what seemed like wooden legs. She mumbled for the thousandth time how unfair it was that we'd moved. "Open your mind, Deanna," I said in tone too motherly for addressing a teenage girl.

"Whatever," she growled.

Dense underbrush crept onto and through the boardwalk. Kurtis and Shyla asked constant questions about vegetation they'd never seen before. We stopped at every pathway sign and they took turns reading information about the wetlands aloud. I looked at my husband. "She's reading," I whispered. He nodded and smiled.

Suddenly, our moping teenager started pointing and calling out, "A bird! It's a bird! Mom, it's a bird!" Standing in the middle of the prairie was a great blue heron that lifted its wings and took flight. Her mouth curved into a smile, the first smile in days.

Since that day, we've seen the wetlands change with the seasons from grassy prairie and dense vegetation to swampland to an ice-encased wonder to a haven for wild roses and tadpoles. We've learned how things change and grow, seen a variety of birds and animals, and come to enjoy our time together as a family. And even our teenager agrees that there is no better place than Corvallis. Where else can you walk from an apartment into the wild?

Larina Warnock is a development associate for Corvallis Public Schools Foundation. She lives in Northwest Corvallis with her husband and four children. In her spare time, Larina studies and writes literature in all its forms, volunteers for social and literary organizations including the Academy of American Poets, and edits an online journal, The Externalist. *Larina's poetry has appeared in*

Autumn Sky Poetry *and* Night Roses, *placed in the IBPC, and twice been short listed for* The Guardian's *poetry workshops. She has just completed her first full-length collection of poetry and is working on a novel.*

Jackson Frasier Wetlands (by L. Dyer)

Look Up!
JILL ALLPHIN

In New York City they say it's easy to spot tourists, they're the ones looking up. In Corvallis, we have our own reasons for looking up—the trees.

Moving to Corvallis from Phoenix in the summer of '78, was like moving from a sand dune to an oasis, but by winter, when I wanted to cry at yet another gray sky, some tree was always getting in the way. Seasons only made the trees more interesting.

In winter, on the OSU campus, in the MU quad, you'll find a towering trio of Giant Sequoias. Push aside their shaggy arms, step in among them, and look up. Suddenly you're alone in a primordial forest. Taste the spicy air. Breathe the ancient scent. Feel the springy earth as through the soles of Luckiamute moccasins.

In spring, across Dixon Creek from Grant Avenue Baptist Church, visit Old Man Willow. Green gossamer strands drape to the ground. Slip inside and find yourself in Middle Earth on the banks of the Withywindle. But looking up, you'll see *this* giant is human-friendly, for in his arms he cradles a lovely wooden deck.

In summer, stroll a few doors north of Grant on Dixon Street and look up. A magnificent Catalpa blooms, an enormous wedding bouquet of orchid-like blossoms dwarfing the house behind it. Its delicate perfume promises a tropical honeymoon.

Finally, fall—the Grand Finale—flies into its favorite west coast town like a sunset on vacation, partying all day long in the treetops. Screaming Scarlet. Electric Yellow. Manic Magenta. Corvallis is ablaze. You are dazed.

Look up! New York City has nothing on us.

Jill Allphin is a study in contradictions. She considers herself a writer, while enjoying her "day job" with Oregon's Department of Human Services. And she maintains that she's still a desert rat at heart, while continuing to live, write, and wander around— looking up—in Corvallis.

Memorial Union Quad in fall color (by Dennis Wolverton)

Oak Creek
NATALIE DALEY

My dogs dream of going to OSU's McDonald Research Forest off 53rd Street, only twenty minutes from home. Delighted to ride in the car, Grendel, our girl dog, vigilantly watches cattle, sheep, and llamas, living miraculously close to downtown Corvallis. Ronin, her twin brother, keens joyously, heralding our arrival in the woods.

We park, and take the first path to the left, Homestead Trail, and thump across the small bridge over Oak Creek. Seasonal trillium, blackberries, or sunflowers decorate narrow graveled paths. A particularly lovely mud wallow entices Grendel, but we catch her before she can sit in it. At the base of a distant hill, the dogs splash around in a much cleaner pond. Reluctantly, they shake off the water and begin the next incline.

My favorite meadow blankets a shallow rise. Our dogs leap the dry drainage ditch to dash across. A touch of rain inspired a few hardy fall flowers to dot the golden field. Pines, firs, and deciduous trees zigzag across the horizon. Dry leaves and needles waft on a sweet fall breeze, disturbing the silence.

Over the next hill and down the road, the creek offers a last shallow swimming place. Both dogs dive in, bathing their paws in the cool water, a welcome respite from the gravel. Walking slowly, a few seeds and burrs still attached to their coats, the dogs stand patiently by the car. Dog treats for each and they rest on the blanketed back seat.

A spray of leaves hits the windshield as we drive away. Soon the forest may be a herringbone fabric of snow and ice. Spring trillium and new leaves will come.

I teach tech writing, graphic design for writers, composition, and literature at Linn-Benton Community College. In my copious spare time, I have small business, The Writer's Shop. I'll write, edit, or design anything anytime, anywhere.

Snowy bridge at Oak Creek (by Carrie Brownell, Blue Castle Photography)

Oh, No, You Go First
LEE LAWTON

ten years ago, I moved to Oregon from Phoenix, Arizona. Twenty-five years of saguaros, cactus wrens, burrowing owls, and dust devils; creosote bushes, thunderstorms, smog, and freeway traffic. Freeway traffic, which often meant an unremitting chain of vehicles, nearly joined at their bumpers, driving at top speed—which sometimes meant stopped completely—as if pots of gold were being given away at the next exit. Drivers so selfish, you didn't dare signal a lane change, or the tiny space between cars you needed would immediately disappear.

Willamette Valley drivers are quite different. At a four-way stop, drivers sometimes spend several minutes offering waves of encouragement to all the drivers around them. At a recent Corvallis road construction site, where stoplights had been temporarily replaced with stop signs, not a single accident occurred during the several weeks of road work. Signal a lane change on the freeway around here, and space large enough to accommodate a funeral procession opens up.

At first, I found this not only remarkable but so . . . polite, such good manners, so pleasing. Now, after ten years, as I follow folks going thirty mph in a forty-five mph zone, or stuck behind people who come to a full stop at yield signs, I find myself steaming. Why do they drive like that? Don't people here know about that pot of gold?

Lee Lawton writes poetry and prose when she isn't working as a chef or indexing books. She loves good writing as much as she loves good food!

Corvallis sidewalk café (by Cristina White)

Oregon State University
SPONSOR

With a heritage dating back to 1858, Oregon State University grew up alongside the city of Corvallis, forging a bond of cooperation, trust, and friendship over the years.

The university that is now a major teaching, research, and public service institution started as a small, private academy called Corvallis College. State assistance to higher education in Oregon began October 27, 1868, when Corvallis College was designated as the agricultural college of the state.

College-level courses were introduced into the curriculum around 1865, and two men and one woman completed the baccalaureate degree requirements in 1870, becoming the first graduates of a state-assisted college in the western United States.

Several name changes ensued until the school ultimately was designated as Oregon State University in 1961. OSU is a land, sea, space, and sun grant university, one of only two schools in the United States to hold all four designations.

OSU has more than 140,000 alumni living throughout the world. Many notable people have graduated from the university, including Linus Pauling, the only person to win two unshared Nobel prizes; Mercedes Bates, a longtime General Mills vice president who headed the Betty Crocker division; Terry Baker, the first West Coast winner of football's Heisman Trophy; and two astronauts who served on space missions.

With nearly twenty thousand students and more than three thousand full- and part-time faculty and staff members, OSU plays an important role in the educational, cultural, social, and economic life of Corvallis. The university offers concerts, lectures, cultural activities, art galleries, and athletic events for the entire community to enjoy.

Teaching, Research, Service

OSU focuses education and research on its strengths in natural resources, Earth sciences, innovation and enterprise, life sciences, and arts and sciences. More than 250 undergraduate academic programs and some 90 at the graduate level prepare students for careers and for life.

Academic programs are offered through the colleges of Agricultural Sciences, Business, Education, Engineering, Forestry, Health and Human Sciences, Liberal Arts, Oceanic and Atmospheric Sciences, Pharmacy, Science, and Veterinary Medicine, as well as the Graduate School and the University Honors College.

OSU is the only school in Oregon to earn the Carnegie Foundation's prestigious ranking for "very high research activity." Scientists at the university receive about $200 million in research contracts and grants annually, and during 2006–07, licensing income from technology transfer approached $2.5 million.

Among OSU's research strengths are agriculture, forestry, climate change, nanotechnology, and tsunami studies. The first transparent transistors were developed at OSU, as was an environmentally safe glue for wood products. The university also is among the leaders in developing alternative energy sources.

Through its public service component, OSU has a presence in every Oregon county. OSU's Hatfield Marine Science Center in Newport, Seafood Research Laboratory in Astoria, and Food Innovation Center in Portland, along with agricultural experiment stations and Extension offices throughout the state, boost the state's economy by developing new knowledge and encouraging enterprise.

Student Life

The university is an ideal setting for students from all over the world to learn and develop skills. OSU and Corvallis are the safest locations in the Pacific-10 Conference.

OSU promotes diversity, awareness, and sensitivity, encouraging an environment that is responsive to the wide range of individuals and groups in its community.

Involvement is important to a university education, and OSU offers more than three hundred social, cultural, residential, spiritual, academic, and recreational clubs and organizations.

The university established its athletic program in 1893, and by 1915, Oregon State was a charter member of the Pacific Coast Conference, a predecessor of the Pac-10.

OSU now participates in ten women's and seven men's Pac-10 sports. Back-to-back national baseball championships in 2006 and 2007 highlight the successful OSU athletic programs.

Athletic participation is encouraged at all levels, and OSU has more than twenty club sports teams and a full intramural program offering opportunities for men and women.

The Present and Future

Oregon State is recognized as among the best universities anywhere in a number of areas. OSU ranked ninth in the world in the frequency that faculty's published research is cited by other researchers, according to a study covering 1996–2006. Separate studies found OSU first in the nation in the frequency its agricultural sciences research and conservation biology research are cited in peer-reviewed articles and sixth in geosciences research.

The university maintains its teaching edge with exciting and innovative educational approaches such as the Austin Entrepreneurship program, the International Degree, the Education Double Degree, and interdisciplinary programs that allow students to combine study in multiple subject areas.

As OSU looks to the future, it is committed to maintaining and enhancing its education, research, and service programs and to continuing and strengthening its relationship with the city of Corvallis and its citizens.

OSU Aerial (by University Marketing, Oregon State University)

The Power of Rivers
GREGG KLEINER

When the world weighs down too heavily the way it can sometimes, I walk the half-mile through tombstones, soccer fields, and cottonwoods to the Willamette and stand looking out just upstream from where the Marys flows in. To know these rivers have been moving for millennia floods me with hope, happiness.

We've been coming here for years. When our children were small, Lori and I brought them to the river, where they learned to skip stones and walk on cobble and watch the seasons turn. In springtime, the nettles and osoberry bushes were such brilliant greens the children learned the true meaning of new. On summer evenings, the swallows swooped above the moving surface with what appeared to be sheer joy, and the children learned how little those birds need to live. We feasted on wild blackberries and giggled and steeped in the solitude the Kalapuya surely knew. In autumn, the maples and willows and ash trees all donned their sequined skirts of shimmering golds, then let go the last of the season's sunlight like so many luminous coins. In the muted grays of winter, we mucked through mud to marvel at the skeletal cottonwoods with their heron rookeries perched high above the river's face.

"Don't worry," we told the children. "They'll be back again, next spring."

"To lay eggs…way up there?"

"Yes."

"Where it's safe, right?"

"Yes."

These rivers will still flow long after we're gone, and our children, and their children, too. It's been a gift to live so close by during these short years on Earth. I hope our grandchildren will sprinkle a handful of my burned bones into the moving water, skip some stones, look across and see a heron taking flight above cottonwoods.

Gregg Kleiner's novel Where River Turns to Sky *was a finalist for both the Oregon Book Award and the Patterson Fiction Prize. He lives with his family in south Corvallis, a short walk from the Willamette River.*

Fishing from Corvallis (by Shadowsmith)

Praise Song in Five Stanzas
ANN STALEY

*a*fter the Rose City adventure—three years in a
    condo, anonymous sleeper with ear plugs and
    parking meter change, with Madama Butterfly,
    Rembrandt, and The Pearl,

I returned to my downtown neighborhood and home
wondering about community, about the way friends'
    paths
crisscross like 9th and Harrison at 5 p.m.
circle like delirious and controversial roundabouts,
maybe meander like Finley and Chip Ross trails.

At the library they still recognized me, at the Beanery
    too,
at the Arts Center, Grass Roots, and the Co-Op.
Tyee was the local winery, again, its hundred acres
held by Buchanans. And at the other end of town
Jackson and Frazier still flowed through the Wetland,
birds chirping and swooping in December dusk.

The exuberant attorney, the PSN IVY specialist,
the psychologist, golf coach, and geologist were
    neighbors again.
College students, graduated to their next lives, left stray
    cats
and room for freshmen parading in packs on Jefferson.
Jake was still recommending movies and music, and up
    at Withycombe
a Playboy and Oedipus followed each other just before
    the Bard

hit the Quad as a musical and quilts reappeared all over
    town.

This town welcomes flower baskets and Farmers Markets,
poems on the Midway Marquee, artisan bread, cheese, and
    beer,
five cycle shops and coffee—never more than a couple of
    doors down.
Hidden-in-plain-sight-treasures, too—a national journal of
    art and poetry,
the goings on at Shotpouch, the rose garden, the
    Greenbelt, da Vinci,
the Neighborhood Naturalist's birding bicycle tours.

Near the Willamette, Coast Range in sight,
luscious, Pacific-tinged sunsets, views of Marys Peak,
a riverside path all the way to Philomath—and forty-two
    inches of rain.
Down along the water, interspersed with the
    bikers, you can see crows
the homeless, joggers with strollers,
    skateboarders, chess players,
Free Speakers, and, sometimes, a woman, alone
    on a bench, writing.

Ann Staley, teacher and writer, teacher educator, mentor, is a Keystone State transplant who read The Pig-Tailed Pioneer *in second grade and came west to discover her own Oregon.*

Corvallis Fall Festival (by Paul Rentz)

Random Acts of Kindness
CRISTINA WHITE

We moved here from San Francisco, where almost every outing involves investing a chunk of time, money—or both—to secure a parking place. One of the first things I took note of in Corvallis is that parking here is plentiful, and a great deal of it is free. The first time we had lunch at Tommy's, I saw, there on 4th, one of those rare sights in Corvallis: a stretch of street with parking meters.

We pulled into a space about a half block from the restaurant and put a quarter in the meter. For that quarter, we got forty minutes. This is generous, especially when you compare it with San Francisco, where a quarter buys you only ten minutes. We added a dime and a nickel to the meter, and got a whole hour for a leisurely lunch.

As we strolled back to our car we passed a middle-aged fellow wearing Beaver Nation orange and black. He turned around when I hit the remote to unlock the Honda. "Is that your car?" he asked.

"Yes."

"I just put money in the meter," he told us. "It was about to expire."

We thanked him profusely and he said, "You're welcome." I smiled and waved as he went into Tommy's, and sent silent blessings his way.

This is a town where parking meters are few and far between, and random acts of kindness, people being nice to one another, is pretty much the way things are. That's why I like Corvallis.

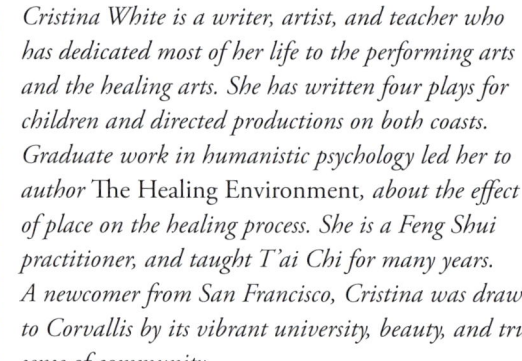

Cristina White is a writer, artist, and teacher who has dedicated most of her life to the performing arts and the healing arts. She has written four plays for children and directed productions on both coasts. Graduate work in humanistic psychology led her to author The Healing Environment, *about the effect of place on the healing process. She is a Feng Shui practitioner, and taught T'ai Chi for many years. A newcomer from San Francisco, Cristina was drawn to Corvallis by its vibrant university, beauty, and true sense of community.*

Downtown Corvallis (by L. Dyer)

Real People
ELIZABETH BENNETT

For me, the word "real" describes many of the people who live in the Corvallis area. They seem to connect easily with their community and their environment. Maybe it's the history so evident in the buildings and houses downtown or the beauty of the place. Maybe it's the proximity of OSU, but Corvallis has a true community feeling.

My first visit to Corvallis was in the early '90s. My husband attended OSU and found himself always drawn back, this time taking me. It was love at first sight with the Willamette River, the open spaces, and the trees. Too, the downtown area exuded a comfortable feeling with its older architecture and one-of-a-kind businesses. Perhaps most striking was that when we walked past other people, on trails or sidewalks, they usually made eye contact and smiled. We decided this was the community where we wanted to settle, eventually returning here for good. Corvallis stole our hearts.

Is it the beauty of this place that bonds people? Rain or shine, walkers keep walking, joggers keep jogging, bicyclists keep cycling. And what a lot of them there are! Surely, being outdoors around other people inspires connection.

OSU is part of Corvallis and certainly does its share of building community. Beavermania turns the town black and orange around game times. Plus, the academic environment builds respect for learning. The entire town gathers to celebrate creativity each year during daVinci Days.

Corvallis, with its variety, beauty, and balance, lives up to its meaning, heart of the valley. It's a center where people can be whole and yes, real.

Elizabeth Bennett lives in the Willamette Valley with her husband, Dan, and their two animal children, Remy and Maui Lu. She has been the voice of Jack in the Box, a Levi Strauss seamstress, a therapist for emotionally disturbed children, an English teacher, and most recently, a house builder. A lover of words and sometime-seducer of the Muse, she has kept journals since she was eleven. Several of her poems and a short story have been published in college and community magazines. She is currently working on her second poetry chapbook and finds daily inspiration in the heart of the valley.

OSU Rugby (by Shadowsmith)

Linn-Benton Community College
SPONSOR

Linn-Benton Community College was founded in 1966 as a two-year public college to serve the educational needs of Linn and Benton County residents. The college is supported by state revenue, tuition, and local property taxes, and it is directed by an elected, seven-member board of education. The 104-acre Albany campus is located just eleven miles east of Corvallis off Highway 34.

Each year, more than twenty-four thousand individuals take a least one class at LBCC, making it one of the largest community colleges in Oregon. Linn-Benton Community College currently offers more than sixty professional technical programs as well as non-credit and community education classes.

Linn-Benton Community College's Benton Center is located only minutes from the OSU campus off 9th Street in Corvallis. More than seven thousand individuals take at least one class at the Benton Center each year. The center offers lower-division transfer classes as well as non-credit and community education courses, and provides student services such as academic and career counseling. The Benton Center also houses a modern ceramics studio and fitness center.

In 1998, LBCC and OSU established a Degree Partnership Program, allowing students to enroll at both colleges by completing one application process. Students in the program have access to classes and services at both institutions, which allows for lower tuition rates and increased flexibility in class scheduling. More than six thousand students have enrolled in the LBCC/OSU Degree Partnership Program to date.

For more information about LBCC, visit us online at www.linnbenton.edu, or check us out at a location near you.

Benton Center of Linn-Benton Community College.

This Piece of This Valley
JANA ZVIBLEMAN

this valley. This land. This small piece of the land of this valley, this fenced piece of land, my backyard. This piece of the land in this valley, this soil. Holding these trees, this fir, pine, maple, breathing air of this valley. Soil feeding this grass, this soil I dig, feeding this tomato. This blackberry, spreading through this valley, this bramble grabbing soil of this land.

Water. This creek, flowing by this piece of land, by other pieces of the land, to this valley's river.

Sky of this valley. This portion of sky, giving this much of the rain to this creek, giving this much of the rain to this soil, of this piece of land of the valley.

People of this valley, neighboring this piece of land. Aromas of their dinners float through this piece of the land. These voices, their laughs, children, lawnmowers. Cars rushing the air of the valley, sirens, schoolyard buzzer, train whistle through this valley. Word pieces bouncing from people bicycling, walking dogs by, throwing rocks of this valley into this creek, passing this piece of land.

Creatures, traveling this valley, through this piece of the land. This heron soaring this piece of the sky, these crows, landing on these branches of these trees. Raccoon drinking this water, fishing this creek. These fish. Deer grazing, cat prowling this piece of the land, jumping fence to the next piece of land. These creatures crawling this valley, slugs, spiders of the valley, hatching in this soil, birthing on this land, dying in this soil, becoming this land.

This piece of land of this valley. This small piece of the land, my backyard.

Jana Zvibleman has been writing as well as drawing, walking, cooking, working, mothering, teaching, laughing, sharing, and more, in the heart of the valley, for not-quite-forever.

HP Park (by L. Dyer)

...Two!...One!...Go!
SPENCER AHRENS

The crowd cheers as we all run to our contraptions in a modified Le Mans start. James and I jump into our seats and start pedaling before I can even get a handle on the steering apparatus. I grab hold and crank it around, swerving between the other vehicles as we pull near the front of the pack. James and I know we have the strength, the question is: will our machine be able to take the punishment that lies before it?

A kinetic sculpture must navigate a multi-terrain course including rolling hills, sand dune, mud pit, and river, powered solely by human exertion. Some vehicles are built with thousands of dollars of corporate funding and shipped to the race here in Corvallis. Others are built locally on small budgets.

My passion for this unique sport started when I was a five-year-old spectator. Watching the race nine years later, my friends and I realized we should be pedaling our own creation on that course. With access to our high school's machine shop, an advisor, and $300 in donations from Corvallis organizations, we began.

Designing and building a kinetic sculpture was not only fun, it was a great learn-by-doing project: fundraising, designing, prototyping, machining, welding, testing (racing), and improving our vehicle. And it was quite a success; we placed seventeenth out of twenty-five. In addition to learning a lot about teamwork and leadership, a most valuable aspect to this incredible endeavor was being able to take something through the entire engineering process, all the way from the drawing board to the field.

Spencer Ahrens is a graduate of Crescent Valley High School and University of California, Berkeley, and is currently a masters candidate in mechanical engineering at MIT. This essay is an excerpt from the one that helped him get accepted to Berkeley's College of Mechanical Engineering.

daVinci Days (by Patricia Thomas)

Starker Forests, Inc.
SPONSOR

Starker Forests, Inc., is a family-owned business established in 1936 when the family's patriarch, T. J. Starker began purchasing second growth forest land. T. J. was one of the first four graduates from Oregon Agricultural College's forestry program in 1910. He returned to OAC School of Forestry as a professor from 1922–1942. During summer breaks he built several homes in the College Hill area. In 1942 he left OAC to manage his forest lands. T. J. was highly regarded for his contributions as an educator, forester, and active citizen. He was involved in a wide range of civic affairs including the Corvallis School Board, the Draft Board, establishing the city's watershed, and procuring Avery Park.

Bruce Starker, T. J. and Margaret Starker's son, was an Oregon State College forestry graduate in 1940. After World War II, he joined his father in business. Bruce's main interest was forest management, by which he hoped to maintain perpetual forest for both public and private use. Bruce, like T. J., was an active citizen. After Bruce's death in 1975, his widow Betty donated land to the city to become the Bruce Starker Arts Park.

Starker Forests was incorporated in 1981 and today holds approximately seventy thousand acres in Benton, Lincoln, Lane, and Polk Counties. It is currently managed by Bruce's sons: Bond and Barte, also OSU Forestry graduates, and a staff of dedicated employees. The fourth generation of Starkers is beginning to take an active role in the company. Starker Forests practices intensive forest management and encourages recreational use of their lands with a free permit. The Starkers and their employees remain involved citizens of Corvallis. They are avid supporters of Old Mill Center, Community Outreach, Inc., the Boys and Girls Club, and Oregon State University.

Old growth (by Dennis Wolverton)

Weather
PEG MAYO

Asked if she thought if it would rain, the old lady, a Corvallis native, shook her head and responded, "Only fools and newcomers predict the weather." That isn't entirely accurate, coffee shops and gathering places are forums for speculation about what to expect and reference to past phenomena. Proving the old lady off the mark, aware folks find the variable climate endlessly entertaining: the antitheses of tedious easy predictability.

Each season is someone's favorite. Winter, with generous rain and little hard cold, allows for guilt-free inside time with warm-sweater temperatures for walks in the parks and along the river. "A snow event" is a rare, beautiful break in winter's mild dampness. It brings out the kid in everyone.

Aficionados of spring glory in riots of daffodils and tulips under the intricate flowers of maples and blossoming fruit trees. Gardeners are blissed out with anticipation.

It is accurately said that living through a Corvallis summer with its easy warmth, burgeoning gardens, fruiting orchards, and star-spangled nights reveals any other climate to be second-best.

There is a glory and an anticipation in autumn. Brilliant color, luxuriously balmy air; and the biggest full moon of the year bathes grateful folks with contentment in the apricot light.

Local farmers' markets overflow through most of the year with the abundance of organic produce grown on the Willamette Valley's excellent soil and nourished in the temperate climate. Riches, indeed!

The weather varies within the seasons, providing conversational fodder and a lovely sense that "something good is going to happen!" Newcomer or webfoot, one can count on interesting conversational material and exhilarating experience. Enjoy!

"I'm the girl who lost her reputation and never missed it." —Mae West
I was born the year the stock market crashed on the cusp of Easter and April Fools. I have been a psychotherapist, crafts person, storyteller/writer, and graphics toyer. My column in the Gazette Times *has run weekly for fifteen years and I have written sixteen books. Life is good at almost eighty. I cannot give you a closing date.*

Winter in Corvallis (by Jeff Watkins)

Willamette: First Communion
LAURENCE P. TAOMAN

Willamette, what are you saying to me? I emerge from your dressing gown of trees and two herons jump into the sky. The slow strokes of their wings take me briefly into the air but your mysterious philosophies bring me back to earth. Your broad body, brown with the soil of recent rains, is wider than I expected and deep.

I descend your bank, touch your cool waters, and still I do not understand what you say to me. Lying down on your pebbled shore I close my eyes and breathe your moist breath. Like a mother or a maiden aunt your murmurs lull me to that place, dark, near sleep and dreams. There I start to understand.

The first nations came down out of the north and you were here. The mountains erupted hundreds of years ago and their ash and stone found their way to you. The wagons of the Oregon and Applegate Trails ended their journeys upon your banks. Farmers and fishermen, young women and old have spoke on your banks. You have collected all their words, as they have walked your shore, navigated your shoals, drank your water, and irrigated their fields. You speak their truth and yours.

I hear all of this in your song, and on the backs of my eyelids I see the nets cast, the boats poled, water splashed on the faces of children, all painted in bright colors. And I feel the waters of my own body flowing with you, north and eventually to the sea. But still and always right here.

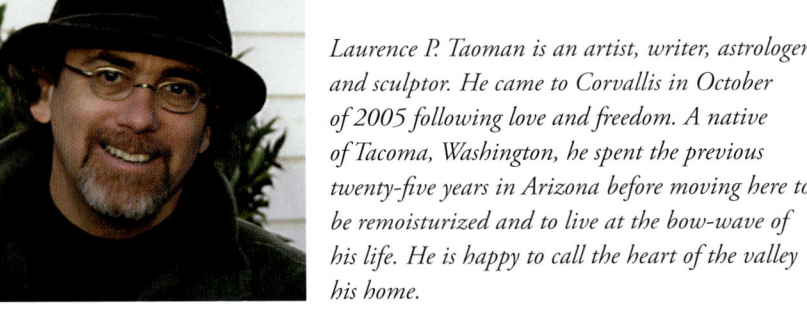

Laurence P. Taoman is an artist, writer, astrologer, and sculptor. He came to Corvallis in October of 2005 following love and freedom. A native of Tacoma, Washington, he spent the previous twenty-five years in Arizona before moving here to be remoisturized and to live at the bow-wave of his life. He is happy to call the heart of the valley his home.

Rowing on the Willamette (by Andy Cripe of the Corvallis Gazette-Times*)*

Town & Country Realty
SPONSOR

Real People Providing Exceptional Service

town & Country Realty opened for business in 1951 and has been the leading real estate brokerage in Corvallis since 1958. The company expanded its reach throughout the mid-Willamette Valley in 1993 by opening an office in Albany, eventually becoming the number one brokerage in the combined Benton and Linn County markets—a position they continue to earn year after year. Their clients and customers attribute Town & Country Realty's success to their long-standing tradition of professionalism, integrity, and commitment to providing exceptional service at the highest level.

One of the keys to Town & Country Realty's success is its stability. Several of their Brokers have been with them for over twenty years, and the leadership reins have been passed only three times since its founding. Another key is that everyone at Town & Country Realty is involved in the local community, so customers can count on working with people who care about their community's well-being.

The company consistently supports local social, educational, civic, and cultural programs. From their own annual *Touchdowns for Toys!* campaign, which benefits local children in need through Old Mill Center, ABC House, and Philomath Youth Activities Center, to the area Boys & Girls Clubs, Corvallis Arts Center, the Chamber of Commerce, Grace Center Adult Day Care, and many, many more. Community involvement remains an integral component of Town & Country Realty's goal to serve their customers and community.

"As Town & Country Realty meets twenty-first century challenges and opportunities such as the Internet and new franchise competitors, we still remember that it's our personal, friendly, and professional service that has provided the foundation for our success," says principal broker/owner Pete Sekermestrovich. "We know we need to earn our wings every day."

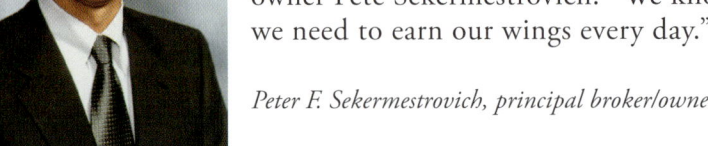

Peter F. Sekermestrovich, principal broker/owner.

Corvallis Office Building at 455 NW Tyler Avenue.

Words Enrich Our Lives Here
LINDA GELBRICH

an elixir of poems
spread throughout town
catches your glance,
slows you down
until your mind pulls up a chair
waiting there
for your feet to catch up.

Everywhere you go there is something trying to catch your eye, to slow you down so you will notice the exquisiteness of the moment in this life that races by so quickly. In Corvallis not only are there rhododendrons shouting their spring colors, the full fan of oaks in summer and the waving ribbons of geese overhead in fall. There are words printed for our pleasure like the ones etched in stone in the courtyard of the Valley Library on the OSU campus. Among the weatherworn lines you read from Narcissa Whitman, The Willamette Farmer, Ursula Le Guin, and William Kittredge. You are reminded, "what a delightful place," "Willamette River like a silver belt," "the dance of renewal," "stay joyous under the sun and moon, in rain and out."

Inside the Corvallis-Benton County Library, poems are printed on steel river rocks below a painting of the Willamette River, by William Shumway. Poems join sculptures and other framed art as part of Alley Art downtown. And if, in your hurry, you have missed these, surely the poem on the Midway Marquee on the outside wall of Great Harvest Bakery will catch your eye. What a pleasure to read these words that slow us down and enrich our moments.

I live in a town
where poems
break free and flow
from art galleries
and coffee shops
from worn pages
and from the lips
of those who love words.

Linda Gelbrich, social worker and poet, has lived in Corvallis for nearly forty years. She works in the Integrative Medicine Division of Samaritan Health Services as a counselor and instructor. She recognizes the healing power of the natural world and the world of words and art. She appreciates the way literary arts are embraced, encouraged, and shared in Corvallis. She is shown with her husband, Keith, who is a nature photographer.

Back alley (by Greg Lief)

Corvallis at 150—Pacific Power
SPONSOR

One early December morning, we pulled on our boots, grabbed our shovels and hit the dirt. Working with the Corvallis city forester and neighborhood volunteers, we were off to plant some special trees as part of the commemorative *150 trees for 150 Years of Corvallis* effort.

Certainly, trees are an appropriate symbol for our city. Historically, the wood products industry and the College of Forestry at Oregon State University have fueled the community's growth. But trees also reflect the future of Corvallis as a center for sustainable growth and renewable energy development. In recent years, the community has taken dramatic steps to establish Corvallis as a leader in environmentally sensitive development. Pacific Power has been proud to be part of this forward thinking community since 1909.

In 2006, Corvallis became the first city on the west coast to become a Green Power Community, as recognized by the federal Environmental Protection Agency. At the end of 2007, there were only a dozen Green Power Communities and most of them much smaller towns than Corvallis. Now, more than fourteen percent of the city's residents have committed to supporting renewable energy from wind, solar, and biomass through the Pacific Power Blue Sky program. In addition, the city of Corvallis purchases seventy-five thousand kilowatt-hours a month through Blue Sky.

Taken together, over the course of a year, the environmental benefits of this kind of support are amazing. Today, the more than 3,000 households and 100 businesses enrolled in Pacific Power's Blue Sky program offset putting 1,718 tons of carbon dioxide into the atmosphere. That is like taking 3,531 cars off the road or planting 337,364 trees.

The way residents here responded to the message of renewable energy says a lot about the Corvallis community. Over the course of the community challenge, commitment to renewable

Professor Annette Von Jouanne leads a team of researchers at OSU's Wallace Energy Systems and Renewables Facility to find ways to convert wave energy off the Oregon coast into electricity. Here she demonstrates a linear test bed created with the help of a grant from Pacific Power's Blue Sky renewable energy program.

energy participation has grown significantly. The number of residential customers participating grew by thirty-seven percent, and monthly renewable energy purchases grew by thirty-five percent. Business customer participation increased by twenty-two percent during the campaign period, and monthly renewable energy purchases grew by five percent.

Committed communities such as Corvallis are the reason federal environmental and energy agencies named Pacific Power's Blue Sky program as the 2007 Green Power Program of the year.

Not only do Corvallis residents use their pocketbooks to promote renewable energy, some are also using their brainpower to develop a new generation of sustainable power technology. At OSU's Wallace Energy Systems and Renewables Facility, Professor Annette Von Jouanne is leading a team of researchers to find ways to convert wave energy off the Oregon coast into electricity. We were pleased to provide $65,000 in 2007 to help create a wave motion simulator to study in detail the effect of ocean movements on wave energy devices.

Of course, we invest on the land (and in people) as well, donating more than $15,000 in 2007 to a wide range of agencies in Corvallis from the ARC of Benton County to a special program at OSU to encourage more women and minorities to enter the engineering profession.

We are constantly investing in our local distribution system, upgrading substations, ensuring more reliability. During 2007, we added special screens to substations to keep birds and squirrels away from energized wires, which helps us keep the power on for our neighborhoods and communities.

And that brings us back to the trees. When we went off planting trees in December, they weren't just any trees; they were special species of trees that fit comfortably and beautifully under power lines and won't disrupt your electricity service as they grow to maturity. That's part of the partnership. When we heard about the *150 Trees for 150 Years of Corvallis*, we knew there was a way to plant trees that make our city more attractive, help the environment, and still allow us to maintain a safe and reliable power supply system for all of our customers—a win-win-win.

As Pacific Power regional community manager for the mid-Willamette Valley area, Doris Johnston is responsible for building and maintaining the company's community involvement through community activities, infrastructure development, contributions, and employee/retiree volunteerism and activism.

She started with the company as a customer service representative in 1973 and has been regional community manager in the Corvallis area since 1998.

Johnston is committed to enhancing quality of life in her community and sits on the Corvallis Boys and Girls Club board. She also serves on the board for the Good Samaritan Hospital Foundation, Corvallis-Benton County Chamber Coalition, and serves as the chair of the Government Affairs Committee. On a regional level, she serves on the Workforce Investment Board for Linn, Benton, and Lincoln Counties and on the Cascade West Area Commission on Transportation.

Johnston and her husband Larry live in Albany, Oregon. They have two children, Marcia and Marty, and two granddaughters, Alyssa and Mickenzie. When not busy working, Johnston enjoys gardening, fishing, and spending time with her children and granddaughters. She is also an avid Oregon State Beavers fan.

Corvallis, A Great Place for Kids
NANCY MATSUMOTO

When my husband and I passed through Corvallis on our honeymoon many years ago, we sat outside downtown, shaded by large trees and agreed that this university town appeared to be an ideal place to raise a family. Within five years, that was exactly what we were doing. It *was* a great place to raise our two kids, and it's only gotten better.

Educational choices abound here from parent co-ops for the youngest, to pre-schools, high quality public schools, private schools, a community college, and a university! Our great public library has a top-notch children's section and children's programs. Outside of school, children can participate in numerous enrichment classes in all fields offered through and supported by one or more organizations or institutions.

Parks dot the neighborhoods, each with an area devoted to children. Creative playgrounds invite activity. A surprise pop-up fountain in Riverfront Park brings squeals of childish delight. An outdoor skateboard park, an indoor sports park, indoor and outdoor pools, tennis courts, and bike lanes throughout the city offer kids recreational choices. Programs through Parks & Recreation and the Boys & Girls Club provide activities and safe havens for children after school. The Willamette River and the trails in the beautiful countryside in and around Corvallis provide ideal places for family outings, while its hills provide great sledding when the snow falls.

While sitting atop Bald Hill shortly after their recent wedding, my daughter and son-in-law looked at each other and said, "You know, this was a great place to grow up!"

It was, and it still is a great place for kids.

Nancy Matsumoto was born in Oakland, California and grew up in Castro Valley, California, where she lived with her parents, two sisters, and a brother. In 1975 she moved to Corvallis, where her husband joined the faculty of the Department of Veterinary Medicine. Aside from her husband, Masa, Nancy's family includes son, Paul; daughter-in-law Rebecca; granddaughter, Elina; daughter, Mari, and son-in-law, Mac.

Fall Festival (by Paul Rentz)

Hewlett-Packard (HP) Corvallis Site
SPONSOR

A Legacy of Innovation

Pioneering technology development has always been at the heart of the Hewlett-Packard Company. In the 1970s the company was on the leading edge of personal computing devices after inventing the world's first scientific and engineering calculators. In 1976 the company sought a new home for the headquarters of the calculator business division, and established the operation in the heart of Oregon's Willamette Valley. Since that time HP Corvallis has become a worldwide hub of innovative product design and an important research facility for the company.

The HP Corvallis site sits on 174 pristine acres and includes two million square feet of integrated circuit fabrication, lab, warehouse, and office space. It is the company's primary thermal inkjet technology development (TIJ) site. This highly successful and innovative technology, pioneered at the Corvallis site, has been instrumental to the growth and profitability of HP.

The site also houses a complete portfolio of advanced research and development and commercialization capabilities for businesses as diverse as digital entertainment and printing platforms. Today it continues to develop innovative product lines for consumers and businesses worldwide. ONAMI (Oregon Nanoscience and Microtechnologies Institute,) Oregon's first signature research center, is co-located on the HP campus.

Sensitivity to community and environmental considerations are evident in the sites' development and how business is conducted. Hewlett-Packard has been recognized by numerous government agencies for their environmental programs and efforts, and employees have a history of and continue to be encouraged to contribute to the community through volunteer and community support activity.

I Learned
MELINDA STEWART

I hiked twenty-five miles in one day
    I worked at a pizza shop; something I never
        thought I would do
I wasted countless hours with some professors
But I made up for it with those who were worth it.
I learned about dish styles
        and textiles
          Tree names
          And Opera
          Global warming
          The psychology of color and how to cook
          Ocean floor mapping
          Film genre
About Darfur and Rwanda
Wilderness management principles and
    cultural resource values
I got a kitten and learned to throw a pot

I sewed dresses and wrote prose, started a manuscript
    and grew peppers and tulips in my windows
I loved and I lost but grew and I thrived
I restored a quilt and worked at Benton County's
    Historical Museum
I made polenta and learned to fry an egg the right way

I lived—It hurt and it was euphoric and it was grand
and it was impossibly difficult.

I lived and I learned all the while.

Melinda-Claire Stewart is a senior at Oregon State University in Forestry. An aspiring writer, Melinda-Claire enjoys historical architecture, vintage apparel design, hiking, and sustainable living practices.

Weatherford Hall at Sunset (by Jenerik Images)

Covered bridge (by Dennis Wolverton)

Central Park (by Paul Rentz)

Avery Park (by Jeff Watkins)

Central Park in Autum (by Sara Lil)

Reser Stadium (by Paul Rentz)

Photographer Contact Information

Mike Bergen
Creative Dialog Group LLC
mike@creativedialog.com
www.creativedialog.com

Jonathan & Carrie Brownell
Blue Castle Photography
www.bluecastlephoto.com
3730 NW Highland Drive
Corvallis, Oregon 97330
(541) 905-3541

Casey Campbell
(541) 758-9528
casey.campbell@lee.net
Corvallis Gazette Times
gtphotos@gtconnect.com

Andy Cripe
Gazette Times
600 SW Jefferson
Corvallis, Oregon
(541) 753-2641

Lainey Dyer
Lainey Dyer Photography
340 SW 2nd Street
Corvallis, Oregon
www.laineydyer.com

Ruth Gallagher
ruthg@cmug.com

Paul Kline Photography
www.paulkline.com

Peter Krupp Photography
425 SW Madison, Suite K
Corvallis, Oregon 97333
(541) 740-5010
kruppphoto@comcast.net

Greg Lief
www.liefphotos.com

Sara Lil Photography
(541) 738-6160
www.saralilphoto.com
info@saralilphoto.com

Paul Rentz
Rush Hour Photo
303 NW Harrison Boulevard
Corvallis, Oregon 97330
(541) 758-3204
prentz@rushhourphoto.com
www.rushhourphoto.com

Shadowsmith Photographics
260 SW Madison Avenue
Corvallis, Oregon
www.shadowsmithphotos.com
(541) 753-3910

Judith Waring Smith
Alsea, Oregon
jubillee@gmail.com

Jeff Watkins
18323 280th Street
Mason City, Iowa 50401

Dennis Wolverton Photography
www.denniswolverton.com

Sponsor Contact Information

Barker-Uerlings Insurance
340 NW 5th Street
Corvallis, Oregon 97330
(541) 757-1323
www.barkeruerlings.com

City of Corvallis
Mayor Charles C. Tomlinson
Office of the Mayor
City Hall
501 SW Madison Avenue
Corvallis, Oregon 97333

Corvallis-OSU Symphony
Carol Mason
Symphony President
PO Box 1582
Corvallis, Oregon 97339
(541) 758-6822
symphony@peak.org

Good Samaritan Hospital
3600 NW Samaritan Dr.
Corvallis, Oregon 97330
(888) 872-0760

Hewlett-Packard Company
(800) 752-0900

Linn-Benton Community College
Marlene Propst, Director, College Advancement
Lori Fluge-Brunker, Publications Assistant/Photographer
6500 SW Pacific Boulevard
Albany, Oregon 97321
(541) 917-4418

Oregon State University
University Marketing
102 Adams Hall
Corvallis, Oregon 97331
(541) 737-3871

Pacific Power
(888) 221-7070

Starker Forests Inc
PO Box 809
Corvallis, Oregon 97339
(541) 929-2477

Town & Country Realty
455 NW Tyler Avenue
Corvallis, Oregon 97330
(541) 757-1781
1117 Pacific Boulevard SE
Albany, Oregon 97321
(541) 924-5616
www.tncrealty.com

109

Author Contact Information

C. Lill Ahrens
754-6044
cclill@comcast.net

Spencer Ahrens
754-6044
cclill@comcast.net

Jill Allphin
jballphins@yahoo.com

Margaret Anderson
Children's author
www.peak.org/~mja

Elizabeth Bennett
elizabethdbennett@yahoo.com

Tonya Claybaugh
claybato@gmail.com

Ange Crawford
541-752-2172
crawford@peak.org

Natalie Daley
The Writer's Shop. Have computer—will travel.
daleyns@yahoo.com

Linda Gelbrich
PO Box 828
Corvallis, Oregon 97339-0828
lindaw@exchangenet.net

Linda Elin Hamner
(541) 929-6343
2hamners@comcast.net
www.cleoandtyrone.com

Bob Harding
Senior Vice President
Relationship Banking Manager
Pacific Continental Bank
robert.harding@therightbank.com
(503) 736-6099 work phone
(503) 267-1284 cell phone

Theresa Hogue
(541) 758-9526
theresa.hogue@lee.net

John Hope-Johnstone CTC
CEO Corvallis Tourism
553 NW Harrison Blvd.,
Corvallis OR, 97330
541-757-1544, 800-334-8118
hj@visitcorvallis.com
www.visitcorvallis.com
Corvallis, the Pacific Northwest's most beautiful college town!

Steve Jones
srjones24407@gmail.com

Cindy Killip
Killipso1@comcast.net

Gregg Kleiner
kleinerg@comcast.net
541-753-0018

Lee Lawton
Right to the Point Indexing & Amanuensis on Call
llami@proaxis.com

John Lopez Jr.
PO Box 1411
Corvallis, Oregon 97339

Genny Lynch
dancinggenny@yahoo.com

J. D. Mackenzie
jdmackenzie08@yahoo.com

Jean Marvell
ART on and of PAPER
(541) 753-6475

Nancy Matsumoto
matsumma@peak.org

Peg Elliott Mayo
PO Box 542
Blodgett, Oregon 97326
pegmayo@riverevoices.com

Alice Rampton
Rampton@proaxis.com

CMSgt Jeff Roy
Jeff.roy1@mac.com

Susan Shumway
8037 NW Mitchell Drive
Corvallis, OR 97330
(541) 740-1635
ambrose.shumway@comcast.net

Sheila Smith
sheilaclicks@gmail.com

Melinda Stewart
melindaclaire.stewart@gmail.com

Sara Swanberg
The Arts Center
541-754-1551
Sara@TheArtsCenter.net

Laurence P. Taoman
Certified Shamanic Astrologer, Writer,
Photographer, Sculptor
(541)738-0378
ltaoman@msn.com
www.laurencetaoman.com

Larina Warnock
PO Box 2052
Corvallis, Oregon 97339-2052
larina76@msn.com

Cristina White
cristinawhite8@yahoo.com

David Wodtke
dcwodtke@hotmail.com
www.earth-service.com

Jana Zvibleman
brucejana@comcast.net

Sunset over Corvallis (by Shadowsmith)